Eastern European Poets Series #29
Ugly Duckling Presse, Brooklyn, NY

Tomaž Šalamun

# ON THE TRACKS OF WILD GAME

Translated from the Slovenian by Sonja Kravanja

*On the Tracks of Wild Game*
Copyright 2012 by Tomaž Šalamun
Translation Copyright 2012 by Sonja Kravanja
Originally published as *Po sledeh divjadi* (Založba Lipa, 1979)

ISBN 978-1-933254-95-1

Eastern European Poets Series No. 29
Series editor: Matvei Yankelevich

Design and typesetting: Rachel Kinrot
Covers printed offset by Polyprint Design and letterpress at Ugly Duckling Presse.

Distributed to the trade by Small Press Distribution
(www.spdbooks.org)

Library of Congress Cataloging-in-Publication Data

Šalamun, Tomaž.
 [Po sledeh divjadi. English]
 On the tracks of wild game / by Tomaz Salamun ; translated from the Slovene by Sonja Kravanja. -- 1st American ed.
   p. cm.
 ISBN 978-1-933254-95-1 (pbk. : acid-free paper)
 1. Poetry. I. Kravanja, Sonja. II. Title.
 PG1919.29.A5P6213 2012
 891.8'415--dc23
                          2011048694

Funding for this book was partially provided by the National Endowment for the Arts and by a generous grant from the Trubar Foundation at the Slovene Writers' Association, Ljubljana, Slovenia. The translation of this book was supported by the Slovenian Book Agency (Javna agencija za knjigo Republike Slovenije).

First Edition 2012
Printed in the USA

Ugly Duckling Presse
The Old American Can Factory
232 Third Street, #E-002
Brooklyn, NY 11215

www.uglyducklingpresse.org

NATIONAL
ENDOWMENT
FOR THE ARTS

# CONTENTS

| | | |
|---|---|---|
| **Good Day, Iztok** | | 5 |
| Good Day, Iztok | | 10 |
| World Touch Venice | | 30 |
| **Plato, Islam, Barnett Newman** | | 43 |
| **Sacred Mountains** | | 73 |
| A Visit | | 75 |
| Clumsy Guys | | 88 |
| To the Snake, to Myself | | 89 |
| History is a woman, let's be gay! | | 90 |
| Ether | | 97 |
| Son | | 101 |

*for Sonja*

# GOOD DAY, IZTOK

From the quiet you unfold a poppy and water,
from black hail the circle falls back.
A pure word breaks through,
annulling all the windows.

The clarity of the world is about to emerge,
painful, yet joyous.
Where do you come from, the happiness
of the drop, that the earth will absorb?

---

I knew but didn't see.
Colorful cool wings
gleamed.
A bang rustled and was mute.

I blew into my hands,
shivered and pricked up my ears.
When will I be captured
by the breadth of this honey?

Heavenly shepherds,
young men on the earth,
where did your women hide,
as you fled into this tree?

# GOOD DAY, IZTOK

Good day, he said, is Sonja at home?
You loathsome comma I'll abolish you again a fat
entropy she is not I said she's studying in the library
   do you want
to come in and who are you iztok aha I heard about you
you hitchhiked to the polish border almost froze to death
you have a brother named jani and you write where can I
sit down to be the least bother you don't bother me at all and then
strange things started to emerge
a glow some sort of a sheaf some kind of little lights
click it became clear that this was
a person whose work threw ahac on his
ass and he gave the space for his book to iztok
then I became a bit embarrassed and worried
I was again rushing things so we ate grapes and sort of
goggled at one another and sort of fondled each other with our
   stares and after a few
moments I was already immersed enough and we dashed off to his
home and he handed me some impressive
sheets of papers in folders and then we returned to
gradisče by then flowing down the same
river and we chatted and sonček lost her
bearings and almost dozed off she was rather
restless while I was wired a journey started to
happen there was an earthquake at night and
I knew what has caused it things started to become clear and in
   the morning after

sonček left for the library I started to read
my first thought was dammit
too bad good work but why are there so many chunks of
my flesh and then my friends some
crazy things started to happen it started to burn
to glow to rustle to blow to boil to pour
bombs all the sand of all the deserts began
to give way I was speechless I just
stared and stared and swam and was moved to
tears I ate sun beams that were
an assassination of my belly my son my
brother my father what had I ignited
of course I hadn't ignited anything more than
ginsberg anything more than apollinaire anything more than
whitman and at the same time none of them or
us the poetry had swallowed itself and
threw itself up it is now pouring down on the earth in streams
I was shot up a few times and wanted
to immediately crawl to my typewriter but there was no
 typewriter
because I had it in my business office at
slobodan's and mira's I hadn't written by hand
for way too long and then I settled down and
stared stared and read and there was another
earthquake in the morning sonček came back and she
was quite restless but before that iztok had come and handed
 me some posters for us to have and I figured it out
that was just an excuse but since I had just barely
got up and was ritually getting
ready to read more of his work and had before that
read schwarz on duchamp and so I just

thanked him and took the posters when
sonček came we all knew what that was all about I
asked her if she was afraid for herself she said
no if she was afraid for me she said no why don't you
drop by iztok's I said too much I had no idea why
I said that and then we
analyzed everything and I realized
I had to at least hear his voice and
called him at home he wasn't there and then
I phoned vesna's mother whom I didn't know at all and
neither did I know vesna her mother thought it strange
but after I introduced myself over the phone she was
   somewhat relieved
after I told her I was actually looking for iztok and I already
   felt better
and I thought there maybe was
no danger at all and I sent sonček back
to the library considering we had both calmed down
by then and then I kept reading and
made a date with her to go to
a movie but she didn't go after all
in the hallway of the library she told me she was pressed for
   time and then
I again called iztok he was at home and I asked him
if I could pick him up and take him to
a movie and he said yes and then we went to the
kinoteka and all the people in there
just a few as a matter of fact because everyone was anxious
about yet another earthquake were very
quiet iztok started to talk about earthquakes and how he slept
naked and he said this out loud I didn't

mind then we watched *la peau douce*
and I was ready to flee but didn't
it was all about maruška and the baggage I carried it was
 wise that
sonja didn't come then iztok and I grabbed a beer or rather
 we both
came to a conclusion we wanted to go somewhere but
since we hardly knew one another it seemed kind of
awkward but at any rate we went to bistro texas there was
quite a scene there and I already was transported so I
started to spill it out telling him how I had been swimming
over him and on the phone all day long just to find out
what was going on with him and that I was mortified for him
especially terrified because he was a rock climber and then I
 was told
that the very same day he and his youngest brother
gorazd had climbed some treacherous rocks that lead to
 the castle
and I realized that my fear for him stemmed
from vojko and franci and ron and
peter and bob and emil and the way I function when at
 times I have
no clue but people still faint and
break their foreheads ring a bell at the
very exact moment when I have an orgasm or
the way I can ram their stomachs and
am inside them even if I am in california or
anywhere else and then I told him to please
stay alive for at least a few days
easy easy make your brother climb with you
then we both came to a realization

that he was not in any real danger that he was not a magician but
healthy whole powerful gigantic crazy and also
gentle and not in danger he wasn't endangered at all
so we shared a beer and then
we were kind of kicked out and we passed a shop window
you are burroughs I said he saw what I meant said yes
burroughs was a black sheep in the family he shot jane and
then as we were drinking beer I told him that what
I had done was just a narrow trail but that he got into me and
    thundered inside me
and flooded me and how he had forged a highway regardless
of what a superb and powerful master I am
and then I admitted to him about the influence
immense and undeniable influence he would have over me
and then my youth was there influencing me simultaneously
it is rather strange I live in the same room
I lived in ten years ago
the same presence entered me as ten years ago
and I proclaim say it with no doubt
iztok osojnik is a world class poet I swear it
until the end of the world and am willing to die for it it's a
    towering wave a lightning
striking across the world's stage the power of the
    slovenian nation
that by now has a recognition of itself
and the sense of its greatness and the slovenian language
    becomes one of the world's
languages striving toward absolute glory glowing there
an onslaught here a march that's trembling bam I'm fully
amazed for the past two days I've been riding on this poetry
drinking it sipping it and reading it

then I put on jim morrison and danced and fell into
a trance my cells expanded I put my arms up I hardly
moved I danced wildly and then we went back to
sonja's even though I knew I should let her be and we
chatted again and ate grapes and I fortunately
remembered at 11pm that it was 11 p.m.
and that I needed to protect her time because of
the exam and I said sonček needs to
go to bed right now and iztok said excellent this is
like finishing a poem at its highest
point when it is good and then we went
to bed and weren't restless any longer
we were in bliss and we talked for a long time and
made love and then I fell asleep on the mattress
on the floor so as not to suck too much of her
blood and the next morning
I was barely awake when I started to talk about iztok's
  poetry again
then I took her to ilirska because of her knee
she fell when we were pushing our car towards a ferry
  in igumenica
it wouldn't start because of dampness
but all of this had its source in mycenae
and then I came back and read again went to lunch and
didn't eat lunch but ate iztok osojnik
and I saw taja in the labyrinth and told her
what was new iztok
osojnik is new irresistibly powerful and then I
went home and zoran pistotnik was there
he had lent me or rather sonček had borrowed
from him a sleeping bag for me

―――――――――――

A regime dissolves
in a mouth. It runs fast on
the soles

of Ion,
what did you see?
Cabinets and

ants,
I swear I saw nothing else. On
which milestone
then, did your eyes
grow so large?

now I'd like to write something that would move up and
down would touch and undulate
fall as a feather falls on the bank and
reflect the clear grace
of keith jarret's fingers on the keyboard
I'm thinking of you iztok
I got scared you are too
frightening and powerful
too strong for me as I am now here
I was looking at kali and at my sun
these dreamlike bodies at pleiada
they never meet with coarseness or
harshness these things don't exist for them
they are floating indescribably in this room
altogether bent and silent
kali is fondling her cheek with her knee sonček is now
calm again
I'm rocking and nodding and feeling the steps of
kali and star how they walk how they
slide on the earth on skin we are at
each other's disposal and sonja is
wisdom the wrinkles under her eyes
vanishing

Tutor-bingo is
clearing up.
There are no more animated

buildings on the bottom.
On chalk: a joint, on chalk:
a spirit,

an outline on
a winter. *Sonny, sonny,*
*listen to the*

*radio!*
Drop down on the leaf of
a mountain goat.

Spiritus Mundi is
a box out of which come also human
legs they lighten like erotica like a trick.
Spiritus Mundi is a trick
a ribbon glued on a car's
hood. I take a little broom and
clean the god's eye the yellow wound is not
icy enough. During this dilemma I lost
170 days before that gesture gathered a trench of
sand. If any
human had a hunch of how all of my
moves are counted he'd break out
in cold sweat. The dilemma was
a blockade my only
true life. The 171$^{st}$ day I no longer had
any rights. I bowed down and entered
the service again.

A leaf—a flaw of quiet
avalanches.
Hey, hey, bread.
Like a coon runs,
like a grove keeps vigil by
a path.
It's going to snow.
A whip cracks. I'm not
the shepherd.

In the garden a
DAY TOLLS
on embers rots a
DANCE one
CLAN burns

---

A piggy bank is a hypothesis.
God pushes a coin into a slot.
Our faces don't
touch.
We sleep with our profiles apart.
I crashed there, you know.
In the field where an elf
on a sleigh is painted.

A surge of the scent of daffodils.

Among the LATINOS a white
SHEET germinated on a chopping block
three fairy sisters came and three fate sisters and
BUTTERFLIES with
GEESE on bread they were all gobbling down their own
GREASE I was awake roaring and
WHISTLING sleds fell into a description of
NATURE it was dripping from
WALLS from the forests and from the forests' branches and
WALLS abandoned this method as not to get
SHOT whispered heather
SCRAP OF METAL sat down on my lap I traded it for the
CLASSICS see where this got us
THREE of us know what is born from the earthquake of the
GRANDFATHER

---

Skunk learn how to play
a flute learn how to
neatly and correctly eat a
STEAK he'll get tired making
compote when there'll be nothing else to
EAT a wild boar is hunting
NEEDLES a boy
CLASPS we're rocking we puff at the clouds we weren't raised
   either on a
SCYTHE nor on
DEW and we didn't
CUT ourselves we didn't drink any blood on
GUMS
BOLTEZAR arrived by train at three in the
AFTERNOON the station was
DECORATED representatives
YAWNED a Kosovar was cleaning
GLASS behind the glass were
LEMONS he was squeezing the lemons to make
LEMONADE the speech was
SHORT

I ate a small
CLOUD that didn't see a
LILY then we all
FOCUSED on a fly which made me so nervous that I jammed a
LITTLE FINGER into his nose who is coming I yelled after
    grass that he's squashing in his
LARYNX came the answer we all agreed he was rather
CRAZY it started to rain in the afternoon and we were all
    in a bad
MOOD a handful is
SOLIDIFYING we came to the same conclusion kinč
RESISTED so we beat him up and locked him in a
CELLAR
HE'S
THERE

31st of October we all had a sliding
EXTERIOR in a sack I threw diapers and
POOP from my eyes flamed
RAGE the doorbell sounded I hurried to open on a
BOARD the gurgle of the
DOOR I heard disguised with
TREES from a
FILM I felt a very scraggly
PUNK but that's not what it was about it was about a
DAM and this sublime
QUARREL that hangs social problems on a
PEG yelled
KINČ he's
EASY-GOING he's feeding on all the light bulbs while I'm made of
STRUDEL and flesh of
STRUDEL and bones of
STRUDEL and blood the civil war in
GAUL tore my
LEG on top of that I'll be
BALD we came to the same conclusion now we were already
  out in
NATURE on a forest inside the
NEEDLES

---

The next morning there stood matriculated
ARABS
ABYSSYNIANS
SPANIARDS all of the above but nobody
INTELLIGENT that I saw and I didn't know what that was all
    about we became quiet
STORMY *olé* my
CUNT is
WHISTLING came from kinč and I promptly began to
    speculate shit and
blood bade some new
PROSE clearly until then I hadn't seen a man bleeding from a
CUNT and I found it a fantastic
TUMBLEWEEDING as kinč kept
VOMITING blood like some kind of a
VALVE and I didn't even have with me a
HANKY a cobbler came running a
NEIGHBOR he also drifted there he was pulling the hair of a
    certain animal which he called a
MONKEY kinč I said now we'll clap our hands perhaps it's
really better
THERE which was also
KINČ'S opinion I decided for a
SYNTHESIS he mumbled

I'm concentrating an explosion,
it unfolds like flower pollen.
At that moment when
the white parachute cuts through the air, when
the night spills between one violet and another.
A pike that hits granite in a silent
film, when this sound remains
behind, erased by my
hand.

# WORLD TOUCH VENICE

It's relaxing to stroll with a beautiful wife in
Grand Hotels
shoving into the soft hands of Latins bunches of
money.
The pillars of civilization are at rest,
marginal touches are legitimate.
We ate honey, drank honey,
thick wines, gold blood.
We enjoyed watching ourselves
in mirrors making love, reveled at the thought
of all who would majestically
touch us.
These beams were hammered into sand,
into us,
for our glory, wife.

we walk into bloody grass
god knows where the night burns now
all of you in faraway places
who are in my service lie down or
clench your teeth
you are my method
my test
don't let me suffocate from the volume of
the victims

Granaries have ripened, wheat.

∎

A cloud hurries as it calms the speed of mountains.

∎

Quiet time, a beast sleeps.

∎

My death is lifted.

iztok you are not making me dizzy you are making me
  a dangerous
light bulb there are two octosyllabics but don't disperse
  yourself
over the language don't disperse yourself with such a force
that the language actually disperses itself
the language here is a very ANCIENT clay
you're skidding the brakes you're a hat but I need no hat
because I'm directly in this bright hallway this ought to be
the description of the situation but that's not what this is
  all about
and yet it is exactly what this is all about
barley and an elephant looked back at the mountain pasture
when he lay down on the ground it thundered
it didn't thunder
it is not accurate what is it then the electricity collapsed
but where did it go it went into iztok and how do
women react just grab a microphone and
ask them they are falling down they are confused and they
cry so that you take your watch off your wrist hah what
did I miss I wasn't late just a small chunk of
life had exploded at any rate you rest with
a woman at night and become human again but as soon
as you crawl back to yourself on mattresses the earth
again begins to be and changes into a flower the flower

cracks open and begins to bloom
you are so damn pure you are so fresh you are
the flower you are the earth you yawn you are
the master the women will no doubt
cry again when reading this but what am I supposed to do why
do they cry because I order them to become
wet such a machine needs to be constantly
lubricated because the glowing air may dry it out I
    was debating
if there was anything human about this is this something
altogether inhuman I came to a conclusion that this
    is something more
inhuman than human

A daffodil lives in wood.
My face is a force upon a man.

Strike an egg, so that its shell shatters.
Let the scent of egg-white, a yolk,
a man and a dog surge.

when kundalini opens I have no clue what it is
a scene on the street a triangle fell under
a sheaf make sure you visit me at istarska #24 where are you
    breaking in
what have you dragged in this didn't happen to me it happened
to iztok then a newspaper vendor stopped beside him and
said excuse me young man may I ask you
something of course you may said iztok who was sitting on
the sidewalk so that all the hippies stopped eating cakes
with spoons but ate spoons with cakes are afghans
really more friendly than persians
yes they are said
iztok the newspaper vendor was pleased
he grinned and went on his way and the other
passers-by started to writhe from the pain in their hips started
    to intertwine
lamp-posts started to sway as if they were
branches and I know
theater is to grasp a branch and theater is
to let a branch breathe and in either instance you let it
breathe nature is hungry for contact we are hungry for
    contact with
nature do you think that when you look at a flower and
    then become
a flower isn't a touch much more than just a touch

your own eyes are now in the flower and they
drink you up like through some straws they drink up your
 arms legs head and
the rest of your body they grind
rolls of dust which is not the dust of rolls fly
water rushes that is not at all water or
dust or small waves there's nothing there and you can then
pretend to yourself if we drew it it would look
just like this you may sink into the most beautiful flower
you squat there like some small beast it is no
wonder at all
iztok feels me beside him when he writes and I feel
him beside me

───────────────

mehur had a weird shirt the first time
he flew off the second time I flew off with this weird
shirt mehur why don't you buy
a different one I looked around where did
franci go god forbid that the brightest minds
of america again drink beer in the europa
coffee shop it used to be this way then for a while it
wasn't this way and now it's again this way
we used to drink wine and now we drink water who is
   working at
the socialist union do I have any
friends there if I had any friends
there I wouldn't sometimes in the evening have such
   wild nostalgic
reveries the dutch wouldn't be all
over me all the dutch get some kind of
money when they grow up
they get 1200 guldens each month while I don't
get 1200 guldens each month no matter how I hurry
the dutch said to me for crying out loud tomaž
europe won't watch you wasting away there
such a lousy income makes me
hide under a comforter when a bill collector knocks on the door
and that makes me
mad how could it happen that those guys with the smallest

weenies on the earth managed to establish such
comfortable lives for themselves
and we haven't andro told me
he had the smallest weenie in the whole army
of course I said to him because you looked at it
from above I too
had a feeling I had the smallest weenie
in the army because I looked at it from above then
andro suddenly got up from his bed and ran for
his painting and showed it to me
but to be honest he wasn't really showing me
the painting he was showing me his
weenie

a master never says
I need to shit
a master never says
a wasp bit me
or
damn a wasp bit me
twice
a master no longer has these
chances
wrapped in symbols and in his
ears which have now become golden
altars he hardly ever lifts a finger
he hardly ever
phones anyone
he just shoots crap and organizes his dough
while his apprentices say to his face
what the fuck at two we
are free
they are duped by him when he grumbles over
the outrageous taxes he must pay

A boy doesn't have
a hat, a hat has
a boy. We didn't bring
a handkerchief with us, we wiped it
on a sleeve, the Bosnian way.
I shook a plum tree, plums fell on
his head which made him so happy that he
crushed them. We put them into
a pink basket.
Then we ran to see the puppies.
Little Paws. It went bang!
as we jumped into
a yolk,
slammed its door and turned on
the engine.

# PLATO, ISLAM, BARNETT NEWMAN

Yesterday evening, at the vanishing point of
Barnett Newman's line,
I was pulled under water. I swam back to the surface
as a dark blue
gleaming blossom. It's terrifying to be
a flower. The world came to a halt. I bloomed quietly
like velvet, as if forever.
Before that Tomaž Brejc and I
talked about the mystery
of monetary accumulation, about the eye, about the triangle,
about God. About the possibilities of reading, about
chance, about Slovenian history and
fate.
Do not touch me.
The way I am, I'm the biggest asset.
I'm water in which
the world's destiny is happening for all of us.
I'm dizzy. I understand nothing.
I know.
At night, when I make love, I
report: first I am a black *cubus*, resembling
marble or granite from a different world,
then a bird perched on its yellow feet,
with a huge yellow beak and
glittering black feathers; then a high

church dignitary. That is to say:
they all wanted to assault me,
me, the blossom.
I am a pure dark blossom,
tranquil on the water's surface.
Untouchable and untouched.
Terrifying.

space that doesn't flutter on hands
doesn't flutter on any figure

∎

bizarre rivers
terrifying plains

∎

sweat wipes milk from forehead

∎

he who truly sees nature
unravels the glove

---

what is this
a wooden staff
catching flies in the name of the word
tarragon opens up into a yellow
slalom a rock pours out
kitsch

a horse runs
an island runs on a horse that doesn't see
a hill

∎

we rock a desert
we don't rock a net

∎

bicyclist's legs
why do you pedal the wheels

∎

soot:
burn away on my palm

―――――――――

these are things not allowed
to flutter
a town is encircled by
a wall and a tooth
a frying pan sits on the castle's terrace
a button of an uniform from a different time
rolls into dust under
palm trees the horizon is
blue and brown
there are no traces of
bells in this
civilization

murmurs are gazelles running on
an eraser
I lift the eraser into the day like
a seashell

．

fasting
gathers in the branch of a river whose
name I don't understand

．

we smolder with brothers
we die in a cuttlefish that is swallowed by
a wolf

I compare a caliph with
a birch tree
the caliph's hat with
the birch tree's branch
we are our own
interpreters whom the whirls
pollinate
a flower where there are
bees and a flower where there are
none

everything I saw humanity may
figure out

■

the thumb is now on a ring
on the ring lives the bride's window

■

shine dream
die sharpness

■

cherries decorated the sweaty forehead of
a woodcutter

―――――――――

my vizier
lay down on the bronze
pavement
stacking up blocks like
the alps to hide his eyes
I throw my scent like a ping-
pong ball it falls into his
garden where the glitter is
blinding

a child touches a perimeter
the perimeter is touching golden blocks

∎

go
calm down the blind man who licked up
the grass

∎

an eye breaks through the first and the second
window

∎

create a divine finger
make a radio

I gave her my black
elder to drink.
She dressed it,
then pulled away from it and tossed it
into the red spring.
Me and the tiger, how we were carrying wine and bread to her!
We barely passed the valleys
in which factories were rising up!
We lay on our bellies
altogether drunk
and a quail next to us was safe.
Goblin, goblin! I yelled,
today we eat the thigh,
Solomon's eye!
The tiger threw cherries at the train.
She was rolling on its roof.
Do you think that rivers
were ever here, I asked?

I am the same here as I was the same there

∎

billboards are the fathers of mud
a whistle is in the song's fist

∎

don't surrender
the outline of a bear's paw

∎

insert volume into my border

---

I rest on sand where there's
a mill
under my
splayed fingers
insects play a game where are you
leaf there is no
leaf on the sun
my body is here
by chance
ascend insects find
an oasis
quit knifing between my
fingers which are all
offered
to the light

only the eyes know why there's rain and the rain's duration

▪

a horse's mane wets the foreheads
of the white and black races

▪

he hasn't a clue what he's doing
he's licking a record with his flour

▪

the image is a disciplined fissure
that throws dust at your body like
a combine

anyone who falls into
an arabian night should know that
laws there are ruthless and
brutal at first one hears *tingle
tangle* from the high stone
walls someone drops a rope
with a basket leave the dates
alone! don't eat them that's
how they stop herdsmen if the rope
is strong enough allow yourself to be
pulled up
for three days I was smiling and
bowing and was just about to eat
the rugs when god
caught me
naked

read through a fable
my last will

∎

god rustles in rocks and bodies
he doesn't see the knot that the grass is making

∎

a mailman never breaks through dusk

―――――――――

I always chewed
on blades of grass,
there was no
chewing gum in those countries.
I caressed his head when he was
nude and black.
Next to us a river flowed out
to the sea.
Look,
a frog and a quail,
then dampness,
then sunset.
And there was dampness,
lights were turned on in the town,
the frogs, though, really
began to croak just as we
paddled the current home.

we don't kiss body's flesh but its
color

∙

gnosis is sifting
sand on a bell
flour on a bell

∙

souls are woven by weaving machines

∙

he who puts up a face knows why

―――――

I'd give all my wine for
an oasis in a crystal ball,
sang the bells. When compared with the poison
of the empire such innocence
hurts.
We rode horses,
caressed birch trees.
We brawled,
we Slavs,
we beat up everyone on the street.
Where are you now,
you strange barkeep on a cart,
the hairy barkeep,
lick the finger!

the sky is ploughed with words
not with a plough

∙

when does a bowl of lentils have its birthday

∙

friday
the thirty-first velvet

∙

lake-dwellers built their dwellings on
bingo
and on green piasters

―――――――――――

Rituals are not yet
named,
the grasses not yet
cut.
A festival of hands: a festival
of glowing human blood. On
this granite pavement,
brothers,
on these glowing
rocks, we sleep. Neptune
protects us, he will
wrench apart
our black
time.

a flower blooms from a recipe
not from god's will

■

god's will is a punished cloaca

■

say: sand of a fragrant mouth

■

a sack of sand is the first secret police

A lake is evaporating,
a peasant carries dry wood.
O, scarf, that was
a turban and a mulatto
in the morning,
remember:
we herded cows together.

---

a snake's neck is the breast of a silent blueberry

∎

we measure the volume of heaven with threads

∎

here death is like a pile of gravel
up higher is not any higher
because the gravel shifts
as a man adds more gravel

∎

on the tracks of wild game

―――――――――

I'll burn the fields!
Wheat is a yellow hammer.
I'll dig black rocks in,
I'll color a shovel blue and
hang it on a tree.
Wasps will buzz.
A wind will rock.
Hay will enter a nose and
dawn will appear from explosions in
factories.
I'll be leaning against the same car
that was my car on
Rhodos.

# SACRED MOUNTAINS

# A VISIT

I

A divine punishment for
Trotsky's pogroms arrives softly and
naturally. Fascism, then, is
nature in its most
aesthetic, its most
supreme rage. But, you are naïve
to believe this rage to be visible. Wrong: it
arrives as a mountain, as
peace, as
an enlightenment in a young deity, as
emptiness, as the one who
breathes. He doesn't give a shit. As usual. He who gives
the least shit holds the key to
the world in his hands. When they shot
Ferdinand—and that was a good thing—Hitler
burst out crying. He threw himself on
the ground from the grace that
had shone upon him, kissed it, moved,
grateful to fate for opening such
a time to him. Tell, Dedijer, who was Princip
really? You said nothing. Who are you,
Peco! And, really: did
the Jews, the wheelers-and-dealers, and all the leftist
pamphleteers accomplish anything? Who are you,
Koko? What is my eye?

I'll stay here and slaughter you all, suck your mythical spines
to the bone for my gain.
I yank the white horse!
I yank Colt!
I yank an open journey to Tibet!
Afghans! I yank your kissing of his
hands from you!
Child! Don't you see that I'm
a Viennese and a cobra, your
restored self! I breathe with each of your
gestures, murderer. I won't
allow you to become a fascist.

II

the walls at narobet's oozed
grease I wanted to eat
snails but was given
suspicious looks why are they then on
the menu besides it was not
the day to eat
snails
I was just being difficult at the table
next to us sat
people from furlania
I'm deeply moved when watching peasants
lunch and dine
I shudder I marvel at
myself and say
"strange!" It's in such moments
I think to myself, you've got no grip
on history and then I hear
singing
"the castle is burning
the count is fleeing
wine is spilling
let blood also be spilled"
wham! they spear me with
a pitchfork
true
the sun I see must appear to them a strange
insect in this heavy
stillness

## III

we rapidly drove to kamniška
bistrica
the air there
didn't feel
irritated I was
free and silent and serene
the forest was red and
brown on the slopes blue
snow I wondered who lived in
the house made from black timber and white
stones my hands were in my
pockets and I turned sonček is home here
she is a wood nymph I looked
at the waterfall water was rustling
but the bark on it did not
rustle when it was hurled
down or because I
spellbound
did not hear it

## IV  *the day of the dead*

yesterday I was in paradise
in the forest with the wood
nymph
we came back I promptly materialized
that paradise into a poem about kamniška
bistrica *that*
*done* there appeared on the horizon
a man born in the year of
a snake twelve years
younger
I had no strength to step into
darkness while making love I was
frivolous I compared other women's bodies in my
arms then it was long after
midnight the day of
the dead dawned we both had a feeling we were in some kind of
conspiracy that
the presence was arriving and it seemed
an angel could materialize or
a message be given for a while
I thought it right to stay
on guard then I preferred
to fall asleep like a log it gets
crowded when the souls
of the dead pour down on
the earth then I phoned the snake soft river
not knowing what it was
all about he asked me to drive him
in my car

sonček had a hunch not to
some sort of a signal
we both thought the car was
the danger but it really wasn't
paradise ripens like
a pear and then falls off a tree
I didn't drive him in my car now
I'm behind my typewriter
the abyss is unfolding again my stomach is
filling up
a dark wild
mass is stepping into my
land

# V                              *a visit*

I'm spellbound and
mellow. One, one
one, three times

one,
a date when a person
is born. Resur-

rection on the Day of the Dead!
I've been such a silly
monkey to be afraid of

this. The abyss is
azure and immensely
tall. I recollect

each and every gesture, each
encounter of the eyes, walls and
paintings,

disarmed, I'm washing myself like primordial
serenity in the moonlight and in
dew, in this

expansive
prism of human
precision

Sonček! I believe I'll just
stay quiet and ponder
rocks and

marbles and the white
roads and who is
who

the father and
the son and the holy
spirit,

woman and atman and
brother, sister and
mother, an astonishing

family. Like
kids we stroll across
the mountain crest, they wink at one

another when I ask them
something. What can we say, I'm
old-school and hard-headed,

and then merrily, as if in
jest, we slide into my
belly, which keeps

breathing, hmm,
it is true, we are the
biggest people in the

world,
PST! Home
at last.

## VI

*2. XI. 1976, night*

sometimes when I thus reflect upon myself,
I truly have no clue who I am. and what it is
I do no one knows. they all
pretend to know, poor
bastards. if I shove a stick at them they don't
say I shoved a stick at them
but say something
entirely different. some shout that I'm some big
*jefe* the others that I'm nothing but
a barbarian who is chopping down the most magnificent
   slovenian
spruce trees, but such statements make
none of us the wiser.
sometimes when I thus reflect upon myself I'm
horror-stricken. I suspect I'm a conspiracy, but
whose? I haven't a clue. I studied myself.
I plucked all my
socialist hairs
religious
hairs metaphysical hairs, hairs with
fuck in them and hairs that make a person positively
grand and kind and hairs
I always keep about me just in case I am suddenly
run over by a car and need to argue
where to be taken. many hairs go simultaneously
on different heaps of hairs and I've typed copy
after copy. I want a good view of
the sea. at first I thought everything will be
clear and dandy after my death but that won't happen. everyone

will stuff their heads with whatever they please
and then run around with this whatever causing even
greater confusion. who I've been and what it was I was
really doing no one will ever know.
I feel sorry for you idiots! mercy!

## VII

don't hustle. if a man
is beautiful and a young deity he sooner or later
enters a zone that interests me.
the exact information doesn't exist because
the dead don't speak but much
can be learned from my poems. my principle
is such: when the last ibn kabdul dies I become
ibn kabdul. when there's nothing left in alexandria
but filth and flies
I become alexandria.
the ignorant flap at me saying slyly:
the sun will cool down and what will you do with your
manuscripts when the sun is gone. explaining the principle
of immortality to fools is the same as
demanding from
a shoemaker to hew
a table. I don't do that because when I walk about
town I notice every
victim who will
ripen sooner or later.
cherries will be red.
summer will come.

## VIII                                    *morning*

I'll have to kill, Lord, I'll have to kill.
Why? I gave water to my
livestock, sharpened my scythe. I built a new
barn, as far as the eye can see
wheat is growing. In town I struck
honest bargains, the grapevines bore
plenty. I smelled the air, it was clean and
clear. Guests were welcomed, I poured them
noble wine. At night we played
cards, sang songs.
I listened. I learned
a great deal. About work, about people, about new
machinery, about food prices. Why will I have
to kill amidst such a clear life? The woman
is crying and quivering in bed. She is not
to blame. This has nothing to do with her. Who is
to blame, God? You or I? What's in it for you,
this blood on my hands, the blood
of an innocent man,
of a tall man, beautiful and as still as
the mountain, whom I
love.

# CLUMSY GUYS

The woman is crying like a dragon because I'm a poet. No
wonder. Poetry is a sacred machine, the lackey of
an unknown deity who kills as if by conveyer
belt. How many times I'd be
dead, if I hadn't kept cool, taken it easy and
been completely arrogant, so I can with my own instrument
blot my
wings out. Fly, fly ahead, sacred
object, that's not me, I am reading
the *Times* and drinking coffee with workers in blue
coveralls. They too could easily
kill themselves when they climb a pole to put up
the electricity. Sometimes they do. Poets frequently
kill themselves. They scribble on a piece of paper:
I have been killed by too strong a word,
my vocabulary did this to me. So don't tell me these guys
aren't clumsy. You find them in all
professions. Any pedestrian can
kill himself if he doesn't know what
a crosswalk is.

# TO THE SNAKE, TO MYSELF

I'm resisting God, not you. I'm jealous of
him with whom you're interwoven. Do you know you're
 blotted out
in something that is not you? Do you like it this way? Are you
a prisoner on purpose? Why did you step inside me,

brother in a green ball? Calm and empty, you
joke and play. When you're the most intact,
I tremble. I'd like to talk to you,
to watch you again and smoke. I dream you come to

me and reveal yourself in my dreams. I dream
I'm rescuing you from fire, like that time when I was
in first grade in Ledina. I dreamed that I was

rescuing my teacher Janova from a fire. I dream that
you come and say, let's go. I'm dangerous with
you whose name I fear to utter.

# HISTORY IS A WOMAN, LET'S BE GAY!

*Treatises on Political Economy*

|

When I'm happy, when I pour it all out, I don't need
a poem, you glow, who are returning to me. You are my
eye. I see how you sleep, I see how you
breathe, safe. You say to me, rascal, how do you
manage to handle thirty people at the same time.
Time changes, the air, walls shift,
when you are beside me. You are my Colt. When I
kiss you I don't wash myself afterwards. Like my father in
Bohinj in 1919. He didn't wash his hands for three
days after the king shook his hand. And
yet. You can erase me just like
a person erases an insect. I am frightened
I'll use you because I know something you
don't. You are the only death after my measure.

## II

God, you are stealing my language and paper.
Work has become your body.
I'm killing you, killing myself, I love you,
I love myself. Give me a footbridge, lightning.
I am blind. I am mute.
I'm lying on sand, adorned with jewelry.
You are under my fingers, under my fingers.
A bunny will come hopping by, or a farmer
rolling a tire. I'll eat
with a spoon, I'll always eat with
a spoon. In the heavens there are shock rooms
and a flame that people blow on
spawns. I'm your parallel man,
I'm your parallel man.
I'm anointing you so that nothing will be left of you,
so that you'll be mine. Legendary is the spacing
between your thumb and middle finger, a silent blitz when
   the thing
falls. Why hasn't it yet? Why do you still
hold me? I don't believe I'm
mortal when I look at you, when I caress you, when
I eat you.

## III

Your teeth are like
a mountain under which rolls the snow.
O, snow! O, Mt. Krn! O,
Lake Krn! I'll turn the palm of my hand around.
What are you doing? I have no skin left. A Malay
is biting my skin. I sent him trains
as a present. Electric
trains for him
to play with. He put them on
a sofa. He's biting my skin.
Steamboats race. A person puts a scab
on a steamboat. A person feeds a seagull.
The seagull eats dung. Hey, spyglass!
I don't use you to watch planks of wood. The devil
is watching them. I'm watching tar.
I'll bite the head off the entourage.
I already have one head on a piano. From
Ghana.

## IV

Ripen, bloom!
I killed you in the air.
I can't go past the law.
It's not placed in me.

## V

You carry me in your arms, but I am
not your arm.
I am not your coat.
I am not your beast.
Your teeth are my soul.
I'm conversing with a dormouse.

## VI

Those positions that allow both
plague and grace,
banks and fluid, the eye of humanity and
plucked eyeballs on
a plate that smell like
fish of fresh air as
eggs fry the class
struggle and have such a wide span—
a lexicon!—enabling them to flirt
with the Slovenian proletarian fate and
trilateral tycoons, who with their
left hands support Brecht and hold,
in their right, a knife, a trident; who
extinguish themselves in women so as not to burn
and are, at the same time, a notorious bait,
a honey of homoeroticism, who play their
innocence so convincingly as if they can't
count to five, just so they can pave
with a panther's speed the road to those in
high positions, these are the evident positions of
tired nihilists, who channeled their
charm into the exact channel
where all charm ceases. Into the shit
of reactionaries smeared on the walls like
the magma of history.

## VII

Those positions that make a woman
the happiest in the world,
just to, shortly afterward,
dry her out completely, that breathe the earth
brilliantly just to stab her with
a knife, that bewitch the most beautiful and
upright children so that they
approach with quivering steps desiring
fire and leaving their addresses
in their books, when their
blood has already been calculated for a long time in
charisma, who howl from the most
terrifying longing just to later
sport their cufflinks, who, in the most
delirious erotic insanity, whisper:
I want you to be, which is nothing but
a black order, these positions are evidently the positions
of the exemplary class enemies who
fancy they purchased
all the stocks of the century and are now
praying only for death which will
magnify hundredfold their
capital.

# ETHER

My hands are tied with rope, on each end there's
wood. The sky is purple and brown.
When I see this, it isn't touching me.
I feel fingers on both hands.
Hear a car driving by.
Wool is sipping me in. I am a sheep.
The air heavy with salt, the mistral blows.
Half-circled arches formed of light
like a wide rainbow from me. I no longer have
weight and perhaps I'll be lifted up.
Then I won't write anymore. I grease myself,
weigh my body down, so I may write.
I only see the first three halos. I can't
look further up because it's all
melting. Everything dissolves, nothing is discernable.
The word is a weapon protecting me from
going there. Now I'm no longer a sheep, I have
an arm, am caressing grass. In my ears I feel
pressure as if I were submerged in
sea water. I can think. I see a house.
Reports of this are a defense against
extinction.

II

Geniuses and angels seep down the people's
noses. At first they seem as
embryos, then spread their fibers like
a chrysalis. I reach down for a cigarette,
clench my teeth and clasp my knees
with the palms of my hands. The Lord of desire is
azure, not monolithic. Silk has been highly valued in
the East because it resembles this air. I have no defenses left.
I'm placed in safe hands. I want to be hungry,
to put a stop to this.
On the horizon that looks like water
but isn't water, there swims a black dog. He
gnaws at my hand. It doesn't hurt.
The black dog is docile. I artificially
create fear. Fear is a work of art.
I am a grave. I pour a bucket
with water over my head. None of this has
any taste, colors have their own
locus, their own sources. Like
ether they inhabit my body.

## III

Sometimes there are cobwebs on words.
Sometimes threads, sometimes salt.
Now there's bark and gnarls and a squeaking
knife. I always come clothed here,
not naked. I pretend
I know how much wind my head can take.
The truth is, I don't have a clue. Sometimes I throw
the knife into a veil to retrieve
the veil. Under skin there's a second skin,
under the second skin there's a third skin.
I see the end of the street. I can count
everything: two candelabra. I see
a lattice made of Sol LeWitt's grid.

## IV

Serpentines are chasing me to sleep,
a child dies.
On the altar there's *chaud d'eau*.
I'll live, pause.
God, allow me to rest,
in a cave,
in the rain.

# SON

I

I was trading.
I wanted to plant my innocence
into my son.
I paid.
I did not touch the money.
He is sending a wolf upon me, a wolf, a mountain,
he'll kill me from the air, in love.
Everywhere I look, he sets traps for me.
He is where I feel the most safe.
I pulled him out of his skin.
I was crazy about my son's skin.
I thought this was going to be a breakfast like
any other.
I put on a record, listened
to the music and was spellbound.
Sand entered my muzzle, therefore I killed his
mother, whom he had leaned on, infant!
But you are outside, let's take care of it now, I
said to him.
He looked at me quietly, holding a snowbell in
his fist.
Let go of that milk, drink mine.
I am your mother. Don't prolong
the issues that are of no concern to us. Give me
your skin, I said to him. And I sucked up

his marrow so that only the devil was left of him. That's how I stay innocent.
The hunted.

||

Between one love and another love there is
a woman whose face I've never
seen. I'm unaware of it.

### III

Bathe in your beauty.
Allow it to behead you.
You are this beauty. She
herself is your big brother.
Don't forget.
Not for one moment.
My ways are
uncontrollable.
Only you or I can
die, or
both of us, or both of us
together.

## IV

Guard my victim under the right
pressure,
you tenants of my death's bride. Knights and
warriors, I've chosen you the best way
I could.
There is no love in me. I am
a mask. When I come close, I come close only
to measure the level of my
preparations. They're
more accurate than night and day. They
must be more accurate than night and day. If I
tremble, I tremble only because
I worry I've made
a mistake thinking of my
humanity. Because each and every book demands
a quote from my opus. Don't
complain, then. I'll
replace you myself if I determine that
your powers are waning.

## V

Killing sounds
authentic, love—less authentic.
Flowers don't smell
authentic, but good.
Killing smells good.
Flowers smell good, red, black and
white.

## HISTORY AND ACKNOWLEDGMENTS

Tomaž Šalamun wrote the poems that make up *On the Tracks of Wild Game* [*Po sledeh divjadi*] over the course of a few weeks in 1976. The book was first published in 1979 by Založba Lipa, a publishing house in Koper, Slovenia (then part of Yugoslavia). A new Slovenian edition was published by Kud Prešeren, Ljubljana, in 2012, just before the publication of this English translation.

Several of Sonja Kravanja's translations of these poems first appeared in the following magazines: *Cerise Press*, *Hunger Mountain*, *Parthenon West Review*, *Rattle*, *Salt Hill*, *Washington Square*, and *Willow Springs*.

Several of these translations were included in Tomaž Šalamun's *The Shepherd, the Hunter* (Pedernal Press). The poem "Clumsy Guys" won a Pushcart and was published in *The Pushcart Prize, XIV: Best of the Small Presses* (Penguin) and subsequently in Šalamun's *The Four Questions of Melancholy* (White Pine Press).